present

A Time of Fire

by Charles Mulekwa

First performance at
The Door,
Birmingham Repertory Theatre

on
Thursday 18 November 1999

SUPPORTED BY
THE NATIONAL LOTTERY
THROUGH
THE ARTS COUNCIL
OF ENGLAND

Birmingh
Providing T

the door

Birmingham Repertory Theatre
Box Office: 0121 236 4455

"The Door is proving itself an essential space for new writing"

The Guardian

http://www.the-door.co.uk

Tickets: £9.00
Concs: £6.00
Standby: £5.00
Mad To Miss Mondays:
All tickets £2.99 for under 26s

Birmingham Repertory Theatre Limited
Centenary Square, Broad Street
Birmingham B1 2EP

Box Office: 0121 236 4455

www.birmingham-rep.co.uk

ARTISTIC DIRECTOR
Bill Alexander
EXECUTIVE PRODUCER
John Stalker
ASSOCIATE ARTISTIC DIRECTOR
Anthony Clark

Tamasha Theatre Company and
Birmingham Repertory Theatre in
association with the Lyric Theatre
Hammersmith present

Balti Kings

A new play by Shaheen Khan
and Sudha Bhuchar

Wed 15 Dec - Sat 8 Jan

Set in a Balti kitchen in Birmingham's
Baltiland, curry wars rage, with price
slashing, chef poaching and recipe
stealing. Pots bubble and the
temperature rises as the pioneer of
Balti is on the verge of being swallowed
by the mighty Karachi Karahi Restaurant
in this brand new production from
Tamasha.

*"the excellent Tamasha Theatre
company"* The Guardian

*"Irresistibly charming and shamelessly
enjoyable"* The Sunday Times

Director: Kristine Landon-Smith
Designer: Sue Mayes

After Dark: Mon 20 Dec

A Time of Fire
By Charles Mulekwa

Cast

Kadogo
Christopher Tajah

Omo
Ali Sichilongo

Ssaasl
Nicholas R. Bailey

Dlrector
Indhu Rubasingham

Designer
Liz Cooke

Lighting Designer
Chris Davey

Stage Manager
Niki Ewen

Deputy Stage Manager
Ruth Morgan

Asslstant Stage Manager
Paul Bamford

Production Credits

With thanks to
The British Council
Sainsbury's plc
London International plc for condoms
Mike Draper Fruits

Introduction by Charles Mulekwa

'See now, I'll tell you something about me. I done strung along and strung along. Going this way and that. What ever way would lead me to a moment of peace. That's all I want. To be as easy with everything. But I wasn't born to that. I was born to a time of fire.'
August Wilson, *The Piano Lesson*

Once, I was assigned to direct *The Piano Lesson* for the Uganda National Theatre and The United States Information Service. In it was the above powerful, if not provocative speech. I could not help, but reflect upon the sort of 'time,' I was born to.

My memory of being rewinds back to 1972, when I was age six. We were made to witness a firing squad, by Amin's military. One of the victims was a sixteen-year old boy who lived a few houses away from our home. In the wars between 1979 and 1986, I had a gun held to my head a couple of times. Now that's just me. Uganda has a seventeen million population. Multiply that. War is a time of fire of sorts. It was, nevertheless, a major feature of my time I had not written about. In 1977, Amin's men chopped leading playwright Byron Kawadwa to pieces. The next generation of dramatists was intimidated during the Obote regime of the 1980s. To feel free to present these happenings is a sign of hope that I neither ignore nor take for granted. I am glad for the freedom. Having made the decision to write about war, it took two years for the story I wanted to tell, to ripen.

When I was drawn to writing, I made a decision to write my plays using the English language. For one thing, there are enough Ugandan dramatists writing in local languages. For another, I wanted to reach as wide an audience as possible. Having said that, it is the stories I tell, their location and the era and experience of the characters that will always dictate the terms of the language. From that, the rhythm will be born, taking the shape that it must. I then directly translate into English.

In *A Time of Fire*, the characters are supposedly speaking Kiswahili. This is because in Uganda - ever since the Idi Amin era - when war strikes, the Swahili language prevails. So the language you read is not 'broken' English: I actually thought in Kiswahili, and wrote in English. Therefore, readers will find that I dropped in a few culturally specific qualities of expression, but I found dramatic means to demystify them just as immediately.

This is my tenth stage play, but my first attempt at a scope of story telling beyond Uganda. My other plays have been specific to Uganda. I am moving into a wider dimension. A bigger challenge. One I have to grow towards, without losing sight of who I am: a Ugandan, an African, who belongs to the world.

REP
Birmingham Repertory Theatre

Biographies

Kadogo
Christopher Tajah

Training: Christopher is a recent
graduate of Rose Bruford College
of Speech and Drama.

For Birmingham Repertory Theatre
Company: Fabian in *Twelfth Night.*

Other Theatre: Christopher began his
professional career when he took part
in Sam Shepherd's *Tooth of Crime*
(Bush Theatre, London). He has since
worked at regional theatres throughout
the country. Performances include
Banks in American Clock (Tyne Theatre
and Opera House); Antonio in *Twelfth
Night* (Leicester Haymarket);
Redevelopment (Orange Tree Theatre);
Jeremy in Joe Turners *Come and Gone,*
St Claire in *Trinidad Sisters* (Tricycle
Theatre).

TV includes: *The Bill* (Thames);
London's Burning (Thames).

Film: *The Passion of Remembrance.*

Omo
Ali Sichilongo

Training: Ali is a recent graduate of the
Central School of Speech and Drama.

Theatre: This is Ali's first professional
engagement.

Whilst at Central: John in The
Treatment, Belize in *Angels in America,*
Aaron in *Titus Andronicus*, Bonniface in
The Beaux Stratagem, Mitch in *A
Streetcar Named Desire*, Claudio in
Much Ado About Nothing directed by
Dalia Ibelhauptaite, SA Man in *Fear and
Mystery of the Third Reich* directed by
Sarah Frankcom, Paul in *Six Degrees of
Separation* (Edinburgh Festival 1999).

Radio: Represented Central at the BBC
Carleton Hobbs Radio Competition
(1999).

Biographies

Ssaasi
Nicholas R. Bailey

Born: Birmingham

Training: LAMDA

Theatre: Astolfo in *Life is a Dream* (Royal Lyceum Theatre, Edinburgh; Barbican Theatre; Brooklyn Academy of Music, New York); Grazt in *Dreaming* by Peter Barnes (Royal Exchange Theatre, Manchester and Queen's Theatre, Shaftesbury Avenue); Laertes in *Hamlet* and Florizel in A *Winter's Tale* (Library Theatre Manchester), Duke of Burgundy in *King Lear* (RNT), Cinna/Pindarus in *Julius Caesar* (Royal Exchange Theatre, Manchester); Prince in *Cinderella* (Contact Theatre, Manchester).

TV: *London's Burning* (LWT); *The Bill* (ITV); *Chandler and Co* (BBC); *Casualty* (BBC); *Heartburn Hotel* (BBC); *Coronation Street* (Granada); *Strike Force* (YTV); *Accused* (BBC); Forthcoming Screen 2 Presentation *Sex and Death* (Hattrick Productions).

Radio: For Radio 4, Albion Towers (C.R.E. and Sony Gold Award for Best Drama), *The Tokolosh, Wasteland, Gaia; The Big Smoke* (BBC Wales).

Film: I.D. (Paranax Pictures); Richard Eyre's production of *King Lear* (BBC).

Author
Charles Mulekwa

Charles Mulekwa was born in Uganda in 1966. He has been involved in theatre since 1983 in Uganda, as an actor, director and writer. In 1994 he attended the Royal Court International Residence, and in 1998 he went as an actor to the USA. As well as stage and radio plays he has also written poetry and short stories. In 1999 he graduated from the MA in Playwriting run by David Edgar at Birmingham University and was attached to the Royal National Theatre Studio. The Royal Court Theatre has commissioned his next play.

Plays: For National Theatre, Kampala: *B'Omusaawo* - co-written with Harrison Mbowa (1987). For National Teachers College, Nkozi: *Legacy of the Crown* (1988). For National Theatre, Kampala: *The Woman in Me* (1991); *The Eleventh Commandment* (1994); *The Last of the Kintus* (1996); *Hands of the People* - co-written with Carol Bateesa (1996); *Where Power Lies* (1997); *Bond of the Knife* (1998). For Makerere Performance Arts Festival: *Onyanygo's Anyango* (1993).

Radio plays: *Nothing Against You* (1995); *Between You and Me* (1995); For Radio Uganda *Kafunda Stage* (1996); *Secrets of Bomoka* (1996).

Awards include: Best Play in the Wildlife Festival in 1987; Best Dramatist Award in Uganda in 1991; National Best Script Awards for *The Woman in Me* (1991), *The Eleventh Commandment* (1994); Best Play at the Makerere Performance Arts Festival for *Onyango's Anyango* (1993); BBC African performance competition for radio drama *Nothing Against You* (1995).

REP
Birmingham Repertory Theatre

Indhu Rubasingham
Director

This is Indhu's first show as an
Associate Director at Birmingham Rep.

Other theatre includes:
For the Royal Court: *Lift Off* by Roy
Williams; *Business as Unusual*; *The
Separation* (Young Writers Festival '96);
The Crutch (Young Writers Festival 98)

For Theatre Royal Stratford East: *No
Boys Cricket Club* by Roy Williams; *Party
Girls* by Debbie Plentie; *D'yer Eat With
Your Fingers?!*; *D'yer Eat With Your
Fingers* - The Remix; *Gulp Fiction* by
Trish Cooke

Indhu was an Associate Director at The
Gate Theatre (recipient of Karabe Award
1996/97) her productions there include
Sugar Dollies by Klaus Catten and
Shakuntala adapted by Peter Oswald.
Other productions include *Starstruck* by
Roy Williams (Tricycle) *Dolls House*
(Young Vic Studio) *River Sutra* by Gita
Mehta adapted by Tanita Gupta (In
association with RNT Studio at 3 Mill
Island Studios) *Kaahini* by Maya
Chowdry (Birmingham Rep Studio)
Voices on the Wind by Tanika Gupta
(RNT Studio).

Biographies

Chris Davey
Lighting Designer

For Birmingham Repertory Theatre Company: *Baby Doll* Other theatre designs include: *Three Sisters* for the Oxford Stage Company (Whitehall Theatre), *Nude With Violin* and *The Illusion* (Manchester Royal Exchange); *Family, Passing Places and Greta* (Traverse Edinburgh); *The Deep Blue Sea, Clay Bull* (Lyceum Edinburgh); *Shinning Souls* (Peter Hall Season Old Vic); *Cause Celebre, Then Again* (Lyric Hammersmith); *Happy Valley, Brothers of the Brush* (Everyman Liverpool), *Candide, Shakuntala* (Gate Theatre); *War and Peace* (Shared Experience/Royal National Theatre), *In a Little World of our Own, Endgame* (Donmar Warehouse); *The Colour of Justice, Dance of Death, Kat and the Kings, Two Trains Running* (Tricycle Theatre); *Anna Karenina, Jane Eyre, The Tempest, Mill on the Floss, The Danube, Desire Under the Elms* (Shared Experience); *Blood Wedding, Grimm Tales* (Young Vic); *Maa* (Royal Court); *Love* (West Yorkshire Playhouse); *Grimm Tales* (Leicester Haymarket); *Just One World* (Aarchen Germany).

For the Royal Shakespeare Company: *A Month in the Country, A Midsummer Night's Dream, Everyman, Easter, The Comedy of Errors, Mysteria, Troilus and Cressida.*

He has also designed for the Theatre Royal Stratford East, Palace Theatre Watford, Buxton Opera House, Sadlers Wells Theatre and the Queens Theatre Hornchurch. For *Method and Madness Cherry Orchard, Demons and Dybukks, Black Dahlia.*

Dance Theatre Credits Include: *Beyond the Wall for Men* (Imlata Dance Company); *Answers From the Ocean* (Womens Playhouse Trust); *Transatlantic Tap* (Dance Umbrella Riverside Studios); *Turn of the Tide* (Queen Elizabeth Hall); Shobana Jeyasigh Dance Company.

Opera Credits Include: *La Traviata* (Castleward Opera Belfast); *Gli Equivoci Nel Sembiante, Schumann Song Cycle, A Man of Feeling* (Batignano Opera Festival); *The Picture of Dorian Gray* (Opera de Monte Carlo); *Faust* (Surrey Opera).

Birmingham Repertory Theatre

Liz Cooke

Designer

Liz Cooke studied at the Slade School
of Fine Art and Oxford University.
Recent theatre includes: *Cooking with
Elvis* (Assembly Rooms Edinburgh and
Live Theatre Newcastle); *Comedy of
Errors* (Shakespeareís Globe Theatre);
The Idiot (West Yorkshire Playhouse and
tour); *The Glory of Living* (Royal Court
Upstairs); *Volunteers* (Gate Theatre);
Disparate Bodies (Albery Theatre); *Tales
of Hoffmann* (National Theatre Studio);
*The Promise, Arabian Nights: the tales
of Scheherazade* (B.A.C.) *Love is a Drug*
(Oxford Stage Company).

Opera includes: *La Traviata, La
Cenerentola, Don Giovanni, Carmen*
(Holland Park Festival); *Tosca* (European
Chamber Opera); *Eugene Onegin*,
assistant *La Tragedie de Carmen* (Opera
Northern Ireland).
Forthcoming productions include:
Spoonface Steinberg (Crucible Theatre
Sheffield and New Ambassadors
Theatre.

Introducing The Door

Since it was founded in 1913
Birmingham Repertory Theatre Company
has been a leading national company.
Its programming has introduced a range
of new and foreign plays to the British
theatre repertoire, and it has been a
springboard for many internationally
famous actors, designers and directors.

As the arts in Birmingham have grown
in stature, with the opening of Symphony
Hall, the achievements of the city of
Birmingham Symphony Orchestra and
the arrival of the Birmingham Royal Ballet,
so there has been massive investment
in the resident theatre company.

Now the company can present classic,
new and discovery plays on a scale
appropriate to one of the largest acting
spaces in Europe, as well as a consistent
programme of new theatre in its studio,
by some of the brightest contemporary
talent. To celebrate this, the space has
a new name and a new look.

The Door's programme seeks to find a
young and culturally diverse audience for
the theatre, through the production of
new work in an intimate, flexible space -
work, that reflects, defines and enhances
their experience of the world while
introducing them to the possibilities
of the medium.

Twins: Amelda
Brown as Mimi
and Anne White
as Gigi. Photo:
Tristram Kenton

Confidence:
Jody Watson as
Ella, Robin
Pirongs as Ben.
Photo:
Tristram Kenton

Down Red Lane:
Matthew Waite as
Spider. Photo:
Tristram Kenton

A TIME OF FIRE

(*Mwotto Wa Waka*)

Charles Mulekwa

*Humbly dedicated to a soul who,
despite the twenty-seven years of jail,
and all else, has lived a worthy life*

Nelson Mandela.

With special thanks to

The British Council
The Peggy Ramsay Foundation
The National Theatre of Uganda

Characters

OMO the student, 19.
SSAASI the thief, 32.
KADOGO the soldier, 27.

Setting

A cave, in Africa.

ACT ONE

Scene One

*Darkness. Dusk. A cave. Visible drawings of the Stone Age.
A radio plays African music.*

*Dogs howl in the distance, prompting the snap off of radio.
Single shot of the gun, also in distance, cuts the howling. Three
rounds of rapid gunfire exchange.*

*KADOGO appears crawling backwards with an AK 47 gun, and
a radio cassette. He is dressed in army attire. He is not a brave
soldier. He is also a small man. Bomb explosions now punctuate
the gunfire. KADOGO disappears, still crawling.*

*OMO enters running. He wears a school uniform. The fighting
can still be heard, but is less rapid now. OMO throws himself
down, prayerfully.*

OMO Oh God...

> *Makes sign of the cross.*

In the name of the father, and of the son, and of the Holy
Spirit ... Hail Mary Our Father – Lord - God... Almighty, you
know all. You know all about me.

I no longer go to church frequently...If you make me survive
this...I...I...I'll be the most church going citizen in this country.
So, please, help

> *Enter SSAASI bleeding from a cut on his head. He is clad in
> worn jeans and a Tshirt with the words:* COWBOY NEVER
> DIE. *He also has a small box in one hand.*

OMO Tina!

SSAASI No I'm not the one.

> *Both are struck with fear of each other.*

OMO Toto...! You are a man.

SSAASI Oooh please, please ...

3

OMO This is the end.

SSAASI I should not have come here.

OMO This is death. I swear...

SSAASI Poor me, now hear swearing.

OMO In the name of the living God -

SSAASI I'm nothing, nothing.

OMO You are everything.

SSAASI Completely zero.

OMO You are a hero.

SSAASI Leave that

OMO I only ask for one thing-

SSAASI Except this box, what you see is the whole of me. Nothing else...Take...

The truth is I prefer life...Dying for a box? Listen no tricks. Completely. I'll put it down here...

(*Does so*). I'll go my ways.

OMO You are a soldier

SSAASI No!

OMO Yes.

SSAASI Do I carry any mark?

OMO You are speaking Kiswahili.

SSAASI There is a war going on...!

   Beat

Really, you also look at me. I'm not lying. I can swear. In the name of my father and mother who are sleeping in the grave. Does a soldier look like this? A real soldier? Ha! Soldier; kill if you want. Me, I'm a civilian. Finished.

OMO The same with me.

SSAASI Finished? Or civilian?

OMO Civilian.

4

Beat

Can't you see that?

SSAASI Not like this. Hard to see...

Beat

But even you, you are speaking Swahili.

OMO To survive.

They laugh in awkward relief...From above, at a higher level of the cave, KADOGO *urinates at them.*

KADOGO Hands up! (*Cocks gun*). Don't move. (*He advances*). You dogs... I said Mikono juu!

They throw their hands up, but SSAASI *can only manage one.*

OMO Toto...!

SSAASI What is this now?

OMO The end.

SSAASI The what?

OMO The very end.

KADOGO Who said speak? Did I tell any of you to make noise for me? You there with your mouth open like a fish out of water; did I say you could talk? You also. You swine with blood; did I tell you to open your mouth?

OMO *and* SSAASI *respond nonverbally.*

What did I say? WhatdidIsay? Answer or a bullet eats somebody!

The two answer at the same time.

SSAASI Mikono juu!

OMO Hands up!

KADOGO Then raise your hands, or a bullet eats you You!

SSAASI I'm bleeding.

KADOGO You are not the first you are not the last.

SSAASI I have raised one hand.

OMO Raise your other hand.

SSAASI I have done what I can. I have raised one hand.

OMO (*Close to crying*) You man! Mister - Sir take it easy with that gun don't you see, if he thinks you are a crimi stubborn, he'll shoot you; then me.

SSAASI You are born once you die once.

> KADOGO *menaces* SSAASI *with gun.*

KADOGO You are born what you die what? Repeat for me... You want death? Don't cry...

You are calling death?

> KADOGO *moves over and kicks* SSAASI *in the groin, who goes down in slow agony.*

OMO Toto, toto, toto!

KADOGO Looking at me like that sends my hand to the trigger...

> OMO *looks away.*

A kick in your things is a simple sample. There is more. Each like a key, to open you up...

Be there thinking you can mock death. (*To neither*). Order ya jeshi ni order. (*To* SSAASI). Repeat!

SSAASI Order ya jeshi ni order.

KADOGO You also!

OMO An order is an order.

> They regard one another, in silence. KADOGO *notices the box!*

KADOGO Oh, oh. Ah, ah. Eh, eh. That box.

OMO Your box.

KADOGO That box is what?

SSAASI Don't know.

KADOGO A bomb?

SSAASI Bo I don't know!

6

KADOGO You don't know!

OMO Mister, you must know!

All three move from it...KADOGO figures out what to do.

KADOGO Your buttocks on your box.

SSAASI I have not looked inside...!

KADOGO Sit!

SSAASI B-b-but if there is a bomb?

KADOGO It blows you for us.

OMO God if in there is a bomb...let it not be a bomb.

SSAASI If I refuse?

KADOGO takes aim at SSAASI, who looks back and forth from gun to 'bomb.'

A click of the safety-catch shows SSAASI the choice he must take; he opts to sit.

KADOGO If those behinds get off that box, their owner gets off this earth.

SSAASI See me how I suffer...

KADOGO You are together the two of you.

OMO No, never.

SSAASI Me, I move alone.

OMO Don't know that man from Adam.

KADOGO Aha! Thank you for telling me. Who-is-Adam?

OMO Adam? Adam is Adam is

KADOGO Whoever he is, wherever he is, he had better show himself... Now! With hands up. Or I fire. Tell him to come out and save his friends!

SSAASI Guy, tell your Adam to come out before we are shot for nothing.

OMO Which Adam you also!

KADOGO You said Adam. You.

7

SSAASI Even these ears of mine heard.

OMO And you think those are ears!

SSAASI When it is my end you open your teeth! We all heard Adam.

OMO Yes, but – yes, actually what I said is: I don't-know-the man-from-Adam.

KADOGO Don't play, you boy, don't play.

OMO Meaning: I have never seen this man before!

SSAASI And me also. Never seen that one.

KADOGO You lie, you die.

SSAASI I'm not lying.

OMO I don't lie.

   KADOGO *does an inspection of them.*

KADOGO You.

OMO Sir.

KADOGO The other empty tin thinks he is a cowboy.

OMO I can see.

KADOGO You are what?

OMO Student.

KADOGO I see a chicken…

   Beat.

   And your friend?

SSAASI Me I have no friend here.

KADOGO You think your size scares me… You think being bigger is a permit for you to say anything, anytime, anyhow?

OMO But it is true. I'm not his friend.

KADOGO Say what each one of you is!

OMO Him, I don't know; me, see my uniform. I am a student.

KADOGO Which makes you even more dangerous!

8

OMO Askari -

KADOGO And don't insult me; I'm not an askari that is just a guard. A small man in the ladder of security. Do not look at me as someone that low. Like a shadow. A scarecrow. Only good for wrestling with the cold night. A watchman. Inside, people are at each other. Outside, the cold is at him. They do each other; the cold does him...

OMO I beg your pardon. Soldier

KADOGO And don't call me soldier!

> OMO *gives up whatever it is he is trying to say.*

Otherwise my next urinating will be in your mouth! Askari? Soldier? They call me Kadogo!

SSAASI That one I will remember: Kadogo.

KADOGO And I know the meaning of it! I may be little, but pull yourself up, if you are a man.

I'll show yourdeadbody how big I can become.

> *Pause.*

SSAASI I'm big for nothing me.

KADOGO Good... And in future, don't walk around with that face.

SSAASI I think I was born like that.

KADOGO That face disturbs my blood.

> SSAASI *looks down.*

This rat claims to be a student.

OMO I can prove it. (*Reaches into pocket*) Here is... (*But it is pieces of chalk that drop*). Chalk...

KADOGO I know chalk!

SSAASI This one also!

OMO Here is my student I.D - you also!

KADOGO (*Grabs it*). Anyone, anybody who wants, can make this.

SSAASI People just forge it like that. (*Snaps fingers*). Times like this, identity means nothing.

KADOGO I want yours...

SSAASI Eh?

KADOGO Don't 'eh.' Produce-your-identity-card.

SSAASI I - I dodo don't have.

KADOGO Search him.

SSAASI Search...

OMO *searches* SSAASI *in the pockets.*

SSAASI Prefer not to carry identity, mine is me.

KADOGO *points a warning finger at him.*

I am quiet.

KADOGO (*Shreds* OMO's *card*). Rebels are using students to finish government soldiers out there. Do you know that? (*Throws the pieces at him*). Tell me why I shouldn't wipe you out?

OMO I don't want to die.

KADOGO You must be a student who comes last in the class. Like an animal's tail. As stupid as an elephant's behind. Farts just like that.

OMO God's mercy.

KADOGO That one was the first to forget about this land.

SSAASI May I say something?

KADOGO (*Sharply turns gun on him*). What?

OMO Keep quiet mister -

KADOGO You know I don't like your face.

OMO You are going to get us killed!

SSAASI The difference is the same... I think I'm going to die anyway.

KADOGO I thought guerrillas are friends of death.

SSAASI I am not a gorilla I'm not a rebel.

10

OMO Toto! Toto! So this man is a rebel.

SSAASI Never been one. Askarrr Kadogo, maybe that one.

OMO That one which one!

SSAASI Him, not me.

OMO Die your death.

SSAASI I have been this and that - never a gorilla.

OMO Guerrilla or gorilla?

KADOGO This one is both.

SSAAS1 Never a rebel. You finish me because of that you end me for nothing. I'm telling you. (*To self*) I shouldn't have opened my mouth... Killing a man for nothing.

KADOGO That is not 'nothing;' that blood.

SSAASI Glass cut me...! I can't even see properly now.

KADOGO Tell one more lie, and you will see.

OMO Perhaps he is not lying.

KADOGO You were also lying -

OMO No, please, no -

KADOGO That you are not together!

OMO He said the same thing...when we met...in here...that he couldn't see.

SSAASI True.

KADOGO Why is it that you think you can fool me?

OMO I don't know where he came from!

SSAASI Who knows where you came from?

OMO Rock Secondary School.

KADOGO Why am I conversing with gunmen who can easily shoot me?

OMO Thunder and lightning strike me if I have ever even touched a gun.

KADOGO How many times?

11

OMO Times? Which times?

KADOGO The gun: how many times? How many have you killed?

OMO I just said I have never!

KADOGO Be careful!

With OMO *done, it is time to work on* SSAASI.

What about you?

SSAASI I'm not a rebel. I don't know a gun; a gun doesn't know me. This blood you see, is my fault. Wanting free things. Bullets were sweeping over our heads, as we were sweeping things from a shop. Five or six of us. Looting. The others got away. For us we struggled over a box. Me and another fool. He pushed me! Into glass. It cut me. Still, I died with the box under the armpit up to this place.

KADOGO Is that box this box?

SSAASI This box is that box.

KADOGO *goes a safe distance, lies on the ground and gives instructions.*

KADOGO Only the one who does as I say is alive. Now you can move your size off,

Mr Big-for-nothing. You box, open that other box. (OMO *sets upon opening it*).

It is only a stupid box, fool. (OMO *succeeds*). Show me whatever is in, one by one.

OMO This little watch…a photograph of some woman…condoms.

SSAASI The things we die for!

KADOGO You will die for your mouth. (*Gets up*). That watch, I want.

SSAASI See him looking; do as the man says.

OMO *obliges.*

KADOGO (*Destroying the picture with his boots*). Thisisthewholestory?

SSAASI I was in pain, blood, alone, gunfire everywhere; something in me told me: 'run!'

That is the me you are seeing.

KADOGO Something in you said, 'run.'

SSAASI Some little inside voice.

OMO I know that voice.

KADOGO And that nonsense of yours said, 'go to the cave.'

SSAASI I ended up here.

KADOGO Reason?

SSAASI Reason?

KADOGO Reason!

SSAASI Eh?

KADOGO What is 'eh'?

SSAASI Eh?

KADOGO Say 'eh' again! Say it, if you are bulletproof…! Why did you not run anywhere else? Like – to your wife?

SSAASI Which woman with a head can take me?

KADOGO Your parents.

SSAASI Dead and buried.

OMO Poor man.

KADOGO Even mine are dead! You hear me?

OMO I hear you…!

KADOGO Dead and buried, not kept in a museum!

A haunted man…

You may now go.

OMO Thank you.

SSAASI 'Thank you?'

KADOGO Leave.

SSAASI Me, I am not leaving.

OMO You man, let me go.

SSAASI Not this style.

KADOGO Turn and go.

SSAASI Go where?

KADOGO Anywhere. Go your way. Go back where each came from! I don't care.

OMO Aska – soldi Kadogo, I do not know you are here. Never seen you.

It is our dying secret. (*Offers handshake in vain*) I promise.

SSAASI Up to you, but I tell you don't turn your back. If you do, you will see.

OMO (*Confused*). What is this again?

SSAASI We are about to die for nothing.

KADOGO 'For nothing?' Don't say that! Are you saying I am a madman –?

Are you saying my here, (*Indicates head*) doesnotwork? That I am: 'shortcircuit?'

'Wrong wires...?'

OMO I didn't say...

KADOGO Starting with you, why are you here anyway?

OMO Me

KADOGO You. You. You.

OMO We used to come here...

KADOGO Speak properly. 'We'...?

OMO Yes, me and ... and

KADOGO And who?

OMO Tina - this is all her fault!

KADOGO Don't tell me about women!

Beat.

What about you, cockroach?

14

SSAASI My friends and me, the others, we used to hide things here.

KADOGO And you also speak properly – 'things!'

SSAASI Goods we had got taken you know; from other people ... Hide them, until we find a deal.

OMO Mother of God, are you standing there telling us You man!

KADOGO You want me to take it you are a thief, but not a rebel.

SSAASI You asked me I told you. That other one said his. I tell you mine, you turn it inside out.

If you don't believe me - that is that. Life! My legs bring me this way thinking I'll be safe in here; but now it looks either you or this pain, is going to kill me.

KADOGO You know nothing about me.

SSAASI Help me, or shoot me!

OMO Don't say shoot!

SSAASI Let him at least do what he would want done for him if he was in my place...

Blood is running. Please stop this blood.

KADOGO I'm not the cause of the blood!

> **KADOGO** *paces up and down, away from* OMO *and* SSAASI.

SSAASI (*To no one in particular*) What is he doing?

> *As if counting one to ten* KADOGO *begins to hum to himself a tune whose menace grows with intensity. He finds the answer.*

KADOGO You!

OMO Me?

KADOGO Help that animal.

SSAASI I thank you my friend.

KADOGO Forget friend! I'm not your friend.

15

SSAASI Thank you who?

KADOGO I am nobody's friend.

SSAASI Just thank you okay –

KADOGO I have no friends.

SSAASI Thanks, Kadogo.

OMO Thank and dance - if you want - but I cannot.

SSAASI If it is dancing, I will dance.

OMO I don't care if you dance standing on a needle.

> *Beat.*

KADOGO Help-the-man.

SSAASI Yes!

OMO I will not. I'm a student, not a doctor.

KADOGO You see this? They cry: ' *yala yala*soldiers are bad, *yele yele*army men have no heart, *yili yili*-they have stones instead, *yulu yulu*-they are born by animals, *yolo yolo*a good soldier is a dead one!' You help them to help themselves; they grow big heads.

SSAASI They let others die.

OMO Maybe, but my head has always been this size.

KADOGO What is your name young man?

OMO Omo.

KADOGO Omo is a washing powder. What is your name; don't make me ask again!

OMO OmoOmoding. Omo is same as Omoding - in short!

KADOGO You are clever.

OMO Even at school.

KADOGO But no discipline!

OMO I have discipline. At school they know me for special discipline.

> KADOGO *slaps* OMO.

16

KADOGO That will discipline you properly. You need maximum discipline. I told you to help that man. Learn; when you are told to do something do it. Especially when you told by an armed man. That is the discipline that saves an army.

OMO (*Close to crying*). That is your discipline, army-type; orders. My discipline - school-kind, teaches me to consider what I'm going to do. What it may mean. I don't do then think. I think then do.

SSAASI I'm dying.

OMO Die...!

SSAASI I'm in bad pain!

OMO Be!

SSAASI What if it was you?

OMO I would be in the pain!

KADOGO Tie the man's head.

OMO He can do it himself.

SSAASI Would I be begging...? I would cry, but who cares? The world can do anything with me now!

OMO I came here for my life!

KADOGO Stop the blood.

OMO I know what you want. I help him, and then we are together. Him...me. I touch him, and you convince yourself. I'm not going to be killed like that. I told you, I don't know the man from Ad ever since, and I don't care about him!

SSAASI Die doing a good thing.

OMO You carry that head for nothing? Can't you see it...? If I touch you: I'm finished, you are finished; we are both finished.

Stalemate. KADOGO *has to work this out...and needs his menacing tune to enable the task. He figures out something.*

KADOGO You, Omoding Omo...?

OMO My name.

KADOGO Have you ever been slapped properly?

17

OMO I'll do it!

KADOGO A slap that changes your life?

OMO Let me do it.

KADOGO Turns you into something you had no plan of becoming?

OMO No slapping, I said-

KADOGO A slap that makes your blood boil?

OMO I'll do it!

> OMO *wets himself, and that is the only reason* KADOGO *does not slap him.*

KADOGO I can make you drink your urine.

OMO But don't slap...please...I'm good...I'm disciplined...

> KADOGO *supplies the orders;* OMO *carries them out. The action is akin to a military drill.*

KADOGO Shoes off!

OMO God knows...

KADOGO Socks off!

OMO Oh toto ...

KADOGO Tie socks together!

OMO Toto, toto, toto...

KADOGO And use on that thief!

SSAASI I'd do the same for you; promise.

OMO (*Fixing* SSAASI, *talking to self*) God in heaven you must be angry.

SSAASI Ouch!

OMO But for how long do you punish?

SSAASI Be kind.

KADOGO No orders from you!

> *Silence.*

OMO Finished.

18

SSAASI That is much better. Let me see…that is the thing!

OMO Toto! Not even thanks?

SSAASI Okay, thank you. What does it mean ... 'toto?' (*No answer*).

Omo, toto is what? Eh?

KADOGO Answer!

OMO Mother...

SSAASI Mother? You mean

OMO Mother! Mother! *Ma-toto, Mom-toto, Mayi-toto, Mama-toto*; what do you call yours!

SSAASI So you come from the east. (*Offers handshake*). You don't look like them.

OMO (*Slaps hand away*). Do I look like your grandmother?

SSAASI Now where did my grandmother come from? I only said -

OMO Leave me! As if you look like a cowboy.

SSAASI Abuse.

OMO You know this is war. A time when you can live or die because of where you come from. Because of the language you speak or cannot speak.

SSAASI But all of us are speaking Swahili in here.

OMO Then leave where I come from alone.

SSAASI In my eyes, all that is innocent… It is the people.

KADOGO Which people?

SSAASI The people who do not like other people.

KADOGO Hard to like if you are hated.

OMO I swear no hatred.

SSAASI I am the one who will never hate.

KADOGO My ears heard very well, and none said 'like.' The word was 'hate.'

SSAASI My body feels bad news coming.

19

KADOGO Oh don't even say! Bad news is seeing a newspaper headline: 'BAD NEWS SO AND SO IS BACK!' And he is from where this 'so and so'...? North... To some of you, we stopped being people; no longer human...we became Northerners - see their eyes - I'm from north! Yes, north!

SSAASI Surely people can come from anywhere.

OMO It is the same country.

KADOGO But "Northerners this; northerners that: northerners *quarraquarra*." So from there you see an enemy, from here I see two.

Awkward silence.

SSAASI Me I have no enemies.

OMO I had no choice. I found myself on God's earth.

KADOGO Two against one. (*Wields gun*). Two against two.

OMO Take it easy.

KADOGO Why the talk? Let's finish each other.

OMO If you look at it I'm an Easterner, true, but my parents did that. Papa and toto. How, is their business... I believe one God, one country.

KADOGO This country bleeds and cries and dies... Everyone's hands are in this mess.

SSAASI That one there, true.

KADOGO Who sent you to tell me what is true, what is not?

SSAASI Nobody.

KADOGO Nobody even knows your name.

SSAASI Er...me? Name?

KADOGO Even dogs have names.

SSAASI Oh yes, given to them by people; but the same people dislike being called dogs.

KADOGO If you are playing

SSAASI Playing? I fear to play with one who has a gun.

20

OMO Then why risk no, nothing.

KADOGO What?

OMO Nothing!

KADOGO Tell where you come from. Without hiding, without deceiving.

SSAASI I'm going to tell you! I'm going to say. I'm saying. Me, no side. Mixed blood.

In fact I speak five languages even.

KADOGO I don't want all that! Place. Tribe.

SSAASI But if I say... I have not forgotten what that one said. That you can live or die because of

OMO But what is wrong with you man? Pulling me into your shit. Every time. I hate you...for that.

SSAASI But it is true. I say, and he shoots.

OMO Then get away from my back!

He shoves which creates a scuffle in which SSAASI *is trying to use* OMO *as a shield.* OMO *struggles to go free. This incites* KADOGO *to have gun at the ready, in case. The three shout. Until buttons on* OMO's *shirt break off.*

My buttons...!

SSAASI What about my life?

KADOGO Try that again, and you will get it! Something simple. You monkeys are still alive because of me. Nobody else. If I decide, nothing can save you. Not even the Pope!Where do you come from?

SSAASI My father was from central, my mother was from west.

KADOGO He is east. You: West, Central, all over the place... Real thief.

SSAASI opts for the funny side of the matter, and finds laughter to show for it. KADOGO adds to it, but from a point of view of mockery. OMO is unsure, but joins in.

KADOGO (*Indicating head*). My here works.

SSAASI Yes, very much! (*To* OMO) He is funny!

21

His laughter is faded by KADOGO'S *placement of gun muzzle under his nostril.*

KADOGO (*For* OMO) If you move, I'll pull the trigger, and his blood is on your hands!

SSAASI Omo -

OMO Don't call my name!

SSAASI I'll not call your name, but don't move - for me. I would do the same for you... That is my dying promise to you.

OMO *somehow does not move.*

KADOGO And my promise is to shoot you, if you continue hiding your name.

SSAASI Ssaasi.

KADOGO Meaning?

SSAASI My name.

KADOGO Nobody is called that. Ssaasi means bullet!

SSAASI It's not my name, I mean...

KADOGO You want me to open your head and find what you mean for myself?

SSAASI It's what do you call it? Wait!

OMO Speak! Can't you say your name? Don't you know your name? If you get me killed!

SSAASI Fear!

OMO You fear your name!

SSAASI Yes! I mean I fear I forget I'm finking! Ugh, thinking...Name they give because something happen to you. Help you also! They call and call, and then everyone forgets your real name.

OMO Nickname.

KADOGO Nickname?

SSAASI That one!

KADOGO *eases gun, walks away, but suddenly turns again.*

22

KADOGO Ssaasi is no nickname; it is your trickname.

SSAASI It is the war of 1967. An army man walks into my father's homestead one day, during the unrest. All run away. The whole village has heard about this long demon. Monster of a man. Mrefu, they called him, because he was tall! Like a telephone tree -

OMO Pole telephone pole.

KADOGO This is not a school, sir.

OMO You are right. Talk man.

SSAASI In those days you had to be tall to join.

OMO Ssaasi!

SSAASI I'm sorry! Anyway my father, hm, he returned.

KADOGO Take away! I have run from danger, why go back?

SSAASI Because of me... They had all run leaving a baby behind, me. The long one has me in his hands. My poor father begs! Promises anything, even if it is to be found at the end of this earth. I hear, the man said children of the enemy would grow to finish his people. He will kill me now, so that his people are free the coming years... And, like that, he throws me into the air!

OMO Toto! No...

KADOGO And this is your ghost telling us now?

SSAASI The grass thatch roof of my brother's hut saved me. I landed there. That helped my father to get me before I crashed to the ground.

OMO Lucky.

SSAASI But like that, my father is seeing a small gun in this man's hands – 'bastola.'

OMO Pistol oh, sorry.

KADOGO Do you want to tell it!

SSAASI Father is wet now. Sweating from here to nowhere; and is begging him, with all the begging in the world, not to harm the child, me.

KADOGO Don't make a song, we know the child is you!

OMO Mrefu laughs.He asks my father to play with him, calling it a game to prove who the father of me really is. That if I am father's flesh, his blood, his son, and not the neighbour's; nothing would go wrong...

KADOGO Aha?

SSAASI The madman shoots! My father shields me - with his body. Again Mrefu fires! Again my father uses his body to shield me. And again. Three agains, and my father taking it three times...

KADOGO Finish your lies, I'm waiting to finish you.

SSAASI Truth only.

KADOGO You said you escaped bullets many times.

SSAASI True...

KADOGO You see fools here.

SSAASI I'm telling true – truth.

KADOGO Aha!

SSAASI Next war, my mother escaped firing squad with me tied to her back. The war after that, three of us through gunfire, we go looting...only me comes back. Last war, our neighbour is taken to the front line. He leaves me to look after his house. Schools close. His daughter comes back home... One day, he returns. Just like that. Some people also; no warning, no message, no anything to say: 'I am coming back,' he finds me sweating on top of her! He shoots one of his pigs as I'm running through the pigs.

OMO You are real bullets, Ssaasi.

SSAASI People who know me know these things, and so the name Ssaasi.

OMO Died badly, your father.

SSAASI He lived another ten years. But those three bullets left him a lame, helpless man. And me, what did I do for him? I dropped out of school. Stupid me left school.

OMO Your brother is he alive?

SSAASI Brother ...

OMO The brother of the roof.

SSAASI This is not party time, this is wartime; who knows where who is?

OMO I think you are a lucky man.

SSAASI I think I'll be killed by a bullet.

KADOGO I think if you give me a reason to shoot you, I will.

Silence. Broken by a dog barking, off. It yelps, supposedly from a kick or stone. The three watch from the safety of their cave. Desperate alarms versus hammering on door. Wailing child. Woman's plea against threatening male voices. KADOGO, OMO and SSAASI draw together...off, a receding man's voice pleading now...woman's alarm again, which is cut by single shot in the air. Silence. Dog barks again. Another shot in the air. KADOGO hits the ground for cover. It takes SSAASI only a fraction of a glance to follow suit. OMO, however, remains in the same position. Watching. Silence from the 'valley of death.' In the cave, the three realise how close together they are, and break up.

OMO That was sick! Sick as can be...What are we doing on earth? What are we doing with our lives? And you know, they were talking... Not crowing. Or croaking. Talking...!

They begin to steadily freak out, in varying degrees. However, all three are quite unaware of the fact.

OMO One day I was born; today, I cannot even sleep.

SSAASI Cowboy never die. If he die, never rot. If he rot, never smell. In such times, I never sleep. If I sleep, I do it on my feet.

KADOGO I don't want to sleep. Commandos don't waste time sleeping. I don't sleep. I listen to my radio all night. Time to sleep, you two can snore here. Me, up there. I stay awake. Alert. Twenty-four hours. If anything moves, death! No otherwise. Shoot first, then think. If anything comes, I will be ready. I'm ready. You hear me? Ever ready!

Three lost men.

OMO Can't this cave crush in; or open up and swallow one...?

SSAASI *begins to laugh...*

This whole idea of death playing with us, like cat and rat - it is chewing me...!

KADOGO *swiftly moves over and sweeps the laughing SSAASI off the ground with a military kick.*

KADOGO Laugh at me again. Laugh!

SSAASI Him; not you!

KADOGO My here works (*Indicates head*). Use yours.

SSAASI I try so hard!

KADOGO I caught your eyes looking at me.

SSAASI Me, I'm – I was laughing at that boy!

KADOGO Next time laugh properly.

OMO Or just don't laugh! I see nothing funny... Only fear.

KADOGO I fear nothing!

OMO But I fear! (*Close to crying*). Everybody fears...

You are saying you do not, because you have a gun.

KADOGO Gun? What gun? (*Rips sleeve and bares arm revealing three talismans*).

Tell me about this! My talismans. All the spirits tied in here.

OMO God is seeing all this Satan in your hands.

KADOGO Guarantee. Nothing can touch me. This, is all the guns in the world. Take this gun and shoot me – if you want – see if I'll die. I have shown you what looks after me. Here!

OMO *is unable to take the gun. He looks toward the 'valley of death.' The other two are also compelled to look toward this lurking uncertainty of, life and death.*

OMO Those guys down there. What if they come here?

KADOGO Five days I have been here. Nobody. Nothing. My peace is disturbed from when you two frogs came.

SSAASI Let's become ghosts!

OMO This is serious!

SSAASI And me! We sing into the night, on top of our voices. They will think we are ghosts. That will create fear. We add one more night to our lives.

OMO Satan.

SSAASI The gang and me, we used to play that trick. People feared this cave, and I tell you the things were safe. If they were stolen again, that was one of us.

OMO Why don't we just pray?

KADOGO We are in a cave, not a church!

SSAASI It is singing that answers anything.

OMO You don't know anything!

SSAASI If I burst into a song properly like this!

OMO God is the answer.

KADOGO You take your God somewhere else.

OMO You are not the first to mock God.

SSAASI God, Allah, *lubale, mungu, muranga, kibumba, were, rubanga, sango, chi, lugaba,* whatwhat -

OMO God is not 'what – what!'

SSAASI He helps those who help themselves!

KADOGO I have shown you my god!

> *Neither is listening to the others from now. Their actions gradually build into an intensity akin to competition. Soon they become gibberish and finally appear possessed!*

SSAASI There is a time for war; a time to sing.

KADOGO I wave this talisman, through the air.

OMO The lord is my shepherd, I shall not want.

KADOGO I invoke all the spirits bound,

From the first to the last.

OMO My heart is full of wrath,

But may your will be done on earth.

SSAASI Moja, mbili, tatu, inne, tano, sita:

Saba, nanne, tisa; habari ya January.

KADOGO Firecourage! Waterlife!

Blood~sacrifice! Sunenergy!

OMO You know I am worthless,

But I know this is not hopeless.

SSAASI Mbere mbira mbulira mwana alira,

Mwana alira, alirira tu wee-tu wee.

KADOGO Moonhope! Starsguidance!

Airlargeness! Windspeed!

OMO Spare us the blunders;

Shower your wonders.

SSAASI Tunge-tunge-tunge,

Tungerere-tunge.

KADOGO Coldhardness! Heatstrength!

Raintears! Rainbowsecurity!

OMO From genesis to revelations,

Your wonders rule the situations.

SSAASI Mpo, mpo, mpo ntema omuti!

Omuti omufuduma!

OMO This is not a play,

I know not how to pray.

SSAASI Twinkle twinkle little star

How I wonder what you are

KADOGO Ancestors, do not rest;

To rest is to desert.

Blackout.

Scene Two

Night. Only the low tone of the radio disturbs the silence. The song is the same as the one at the beginning of the play. The radio is visible, but no sign of KADOGO. OMO *and* SSAASI *at the same level of the cave.* OMO *is lying down.* SSAASI *is seated, blowing a condom.*

SSAASI What do you think?

OMO No - have you ever heard the word 'no'? No!

SSAASI This is our chance!

OMO Better safe, than sorry.

SSAASI I am cowboy; be a ninja.

OMO Simple. Don't trouble 'trouble.'

SSAASI No hero in you at all?

OMO I am a super-coward.

SSAASI It is now up to us.

OMO There is no 'us'…!

SSAASI What is your problem?

OMO I hate the way I am so shaken.

SSAASI In wartime, that is normal.

OMO Normal…watching that man being dragged to his end!

SSAASI Every dog, its day.

OMO I was wanting to help…

SSAASI Let us help us now – now!

OMO Too dangerous.

SSAASI Right from birth, danger and me, we keep close company. Where one is, the other is present. One is the other.I am danger. Danger is me.

OMO No danger like death.

SSAASI Each war, M Death and me came face to face. We know each other well by now. Death knows me, I know him.

I have seen what he can do. The power he has. For thirty-two years, he passes me...this time I'll die...

OMO Your Mr Death told you this?

SSAASI Let me tell you who Death is. Death is the people of this world.

(*Looks to where* KADOGO *is*). I have met mine.

OMO You are still alive.

SSAASI Something in him hates me! I wonder why he has not killed me yet? In my bones, I can finish him! But a man who urinates on people... And that gun! He has a gun.

OMO He does. Now leave me. My body is gone. (*Takes sleeping position*).

SSAASI What about escape?

OMO That radio...!

SSAASI He is using it to fool us.

OMO You heard the man's orders.

SSAASI You want to be his fool.

OMO I don't want to be yours.

SSAASI That little man must be dead asleep.

OMO You are on your own.

SSAASI I'll leave you here.

OMO My greetings to the dead.

SSAASI He won't shoot me!

OMO Die, if you want! Alone.

SSAASI He is asleep.

OMO Why keep saying that? How do you know?

SSAASI He listened to the news, I could hear him. Now the music, I cannot hear him.

OMO No problem for me there.

SSAASI Radios play themselves... People use radios to make thieves think they are at home. Listen to me! I know that trick.

30

OMO Good luck.

SSAASI Don't sleep on this luck!

OMO The man might not even be where you think.

SSAASI Here is the plan: together, we go…quietly. I grab the gun. You hit him. Hard.

OMO Why should I trust the gun in your hands?

SSAASI Okay, you the gun, I smash him. To nothing.

OMO Why should you trust the gun in my hands?

SSAASI Trust me.

OMO I don't know you.

SSAASI Trust you.

OMO You-don't-know-me.

> *Silence. Radio is still playing.* SSAASI *makes a decision.*

SSAASI Can you keep a secret?

(OMO *gives no reply*). Omo.

OMO Find some sleep!

SSAASI Omoding.

OMO Don't disturb. Dreaming time.

SSAASI Trust is risk.

OMO Dreaming of Tina.

SSAASI Let us go and settle things with the little man.

OMO If it was a dark night maybe. Moon is out!

> OMO *settles for sleep;* SSAASI *makes a very important decision.*

SSAASI You can keep a secret - I hope. (*No reply*). I'm going to open myself to you...Can you keep a secret? (*No reply*). Serious, very deep secret, can you keep it?

> Hide it between the buttocks and die with it - no matter what? (*Ensures* KADOGO *is not by any chance 'spying,' draws an identity card from inside his thigh, but still gets no reply*).

People are not what you think... My real name is –

But OMO *is gone, with sleep.*

All you know is toto...

Looks again. KADOGO *is there. He hurriedly hides the card in his back pocket, and takes sleeping position like a child discovered by parents at official sleeping time.* KADOGO *approaches, gun in hand. What is actually happening is that* KADOGO *is sleep-walking. He ventures into a coup, where he is the 'hero.' Radio is still playing.*

KADOGO: Your Excellency, I salute you in the name of death. Come out of the closet. It's only a little man called Kadogo... Do not try anything General Milambo: outside is a battalion of boys, waiting like hungry hyenas!

Excellency, look me in the eyes... We die like insects, but you refuse to end a war, from which you are hiding! I am the one who changes all that. Military command has begged me to be life president. But I say ten years, only. Then, erections – I mean elections! Reasons for ending you: not one or ten or a hundred, but nine reasons. Nine I want this nation to remember: (*Counting off his fingers*).

You are a dictator.

To end the war.

Nobody knows your parents.

The name Milambo means dead bodies.

First class womaniser.

Save nation from wailing.

Dicta already said that one, er...what is the word – terrorist!

Eight... I have forgotten.

Nine: you shot, and killed the last president!

Is that fear on your face? I'll be kind: once, twice, thrice...

The counting above denotes the shooting. No gun shots. He enacts shooting with each number. He returns to his sleeping position.

Blackout.

32

Scene Three

There is a struggle between OMO *and* SSAASI, *below.* OMO *physically manhandles* SSAASI, *who would rather not fight back.* KADOGO *wakes, gun at the ready.*

OMO Kill me, you bad man.

KADOGO What is that?

SSAASI I'm sorry.

KADOGO (*Goes to them*). I'm asking!

OMO I want this man to end my life.

SSAASI Omo, Omo, have you ever been wrong? I accept my mistake...

OMO We'll fight until the sun goes down.

SSAASI Beat if you want. I cannot fight.

KADOGO (*Cocks gun, they stop*). Maggots. Jiggers. Rubbish. Vomit!

SSAASI I wronged him.

OMO He tried to climb me!

KADOGO Repeat for me!

OMO People! Yesterday I risk with your wound. Today, you try to tamper with my behind.

That is how you thank me? Thank you!

SSAASI What can convince you that I'm sorry?

KADOGO Just tell why you behaved that way? Animal.

SSAASI Jail. Bad experience I had there... (*Breaks down*). I fought with all my life!

But...they overpowered me.

KADOGO And...you... Go to that boy!

Shoves SSAASI *towards* OMO.

33

SSAASI I'm going to the boy!

KADOGO Look at his face. Close. Closer. Look at that face. Look. Hard. Until your eyes pain. You saw his face among those prisoners?

OMO My face has always been on my head!

SSAASI Bad dream I swear!

KADOGO Dream? In my dream, someone bigger than you – the president got shot.

Shall we all just do anything we dream?

SSAASI I am...so wrong!

OMO Wrong is nice. You are criminal.

KADOGO Criminals down! On your fours, like an animal. That is an order.

    SSAASI *follows each order.*

Bark, dog, bark... Moo, cow, moo... Good. Goat... Hegoat on heat; I want that. More, more, more! Ha, ha, Omo, this animal is a real animal!

SSAASI Omo, I cry to you, tell him nothing happened.

OMO Never be that animalistic again.

SSAASI To my grave, never.

OMO Kadogo, nothing happened. I woke up. Then also, the man is sorry.

KADOGO This is my territory! I'm not ordinary in here – like you.

I, am the commander in chief. I, give the orders. Ssaasi, is right now before the military tribunal.

I, am not doing this for you... This thief is here telling me dreams, 'bad dreams.' I should shoot him, if so.

SSAASI But you are not going to shoot -

OMO Toto! Don't challenge the man!

SSAASI Not that! There is a ceasefire.

KADOGO Ho! (*Runs to cover exit*). Ceasefire? How did you know that? Quickly.

SSAASI Your radio, last night. You listened to the news. I could hear.

OMO Is that why I have heard no gunfire since sunrise?

KADOGO You want to hear it?

OMO Not on me!

SSAASI Omo!

OMO Sorry, just no.

KADOGO Ssaasi, you thief, you think so called ceasefire matters? That it rules me?

In here, I rule! Ceasefire, or no ceasefire... Lie down if you do not want to meet the dead. Now!

> SSAASI *and* OMO *hit the ground.*

Maybe you know of a soldier called Hondo, maybe you don't.

SSAASI Don't know Hondo the soldier, but I know the name and the meaning.

OMO What is the meaning, Ssaasi?

> SSAASI *is unsure whether to say or not.*

KADOGO Tell him.

SSAASI Hondo means war.

KADOGO War. Hondo was war on two legs. Last war, Hondo shot a boy for a cigarette. Hondo wants a smoke, boy asks for money. Hondo says 'no money.' Boy insists 'to die from poverty, better to die from a bullet.' Hondo gives him his wish. One! In the head...during a cease-fire... That boy's dead body said nothing. If I shot you now, nothing more. Dead bodies don't talk. Ceasefire... Just words... Men like Hondo, or even me, can cease a ceasefire.

KADOGO Up! Not you, pumpkin head, Omo. Ssaasi, stay down.

OMO (*Gets up*). I'm thankful.

KADOGO Hondo's victim was running.

OMO I'm running nowhere!

KADOGO Good. I can see you are trying to live. Omo, promoted. Vice to me.

Come to your head. Salute me. Vice, take this belt; tie that POW. Tietheman.

SSAASI Look at this boy. You are now standing there for what? An order is an order.

KADOGO Tie the man before the animal in his eyes bursts out!

OMO *ties* SSAASI *up.*

Ssaasi, I don't like you thinking two cocks do well in the same yard.

SSAASI Your cock is more cock than my cock. I have no cock. Yours is the cockiest cock.

The only cock.

OMO The man has run out of cocks.

KADOGO I really hope so. Trying to scare me - with cease-fire.

SSAASI The radio.

KADOGO I know the radio said! It is my radio. I was listening to it. The news claimed the government and rebels are to sign a peace agreement today. I always listen to it. Why then do you have to repeat it to me? Don't tell me, I will tell you: because you think you are a 'cowboy.'

SSAASI I am nothing.

KADOGO Because you want me to know that you know. Because you think if you make me know that I know that you know, then you will have some power - over me. Be cowboy, if you think a cowboy shits nails.

SSAASI I remain nothing.

KADOGO That's not what I see! I see a 'cowboy.' Advertised.

SSAASI Oh, this silly Tshirt. I don't like it. Might have been a gift. Could be stolen even.

Looted I think. Borrowed. I would never buy something like this. Not my style. I don't care about this lousy T-shirt anyway.

KADOGO If I tell Omo to tear it off, don't cry.

SSAASI I never cry me.

KADOGO Omo, do it.

OMO *hesitates.*

SSAASI Which school did you go to? Do as he says!

OMO *goes over and starts to rip the Tshirt off.*

Tear. It is just a T shirt. Tear. If my life is in there. Tear. I would do the same for you.

That is the spirit boy ... that is the way ... I would do the same for you... Tear!

KADOGO I still see the cowboy.

OMO To be fair I see a halfnaked man.

KADOGO Become his lawyer. This started with you, Mr pleader. The way you were, if you had the gun, he would be dead before anyone finishes saying ceasefire! Something I'll believe when it happens.

OMO Don't say the cease-fire is a joke!

KADOGO Look at it: President Milambo, Rebel leader Mukamtagara. A mad general, against a rebel sick in the head. Both are gunmen. They believe in war, as the only way. As they finish theirs, I want to finish this small one. Order of command: Omo, slap Ssaasi for me.

OMO No.

KADOGO Don't worry, I am here.

OMO No!

SSAASI What do you mean no?

OMO What do I mean no? I mean no!

SSAASI Slap! An order is an order. Slap me.

OMO I don't slap people!

SSAASI Imagine dying for a slap. The dead will laugh at us.

37

OMO Crazy teacher slapped my brother in school; up to today the boy has one ear. The other ear, deaf.

SSAASI Deafness is nothing. Make me deaf, but slap.

OMO Slaps scare me!

SSAASI Not me!

OMO Slap yourself! If again you ask me to slap you...I will ...kick you where it hurts – where you were kicked.

SSAASI Tough is tough. Slap!

KADOGO Saint Omoding fears slaps. We shall not slap. But cowboy claims toughness. Be tough. We have seen men tough and willing to die for what they believe in... But there are others tough and willing to kill them.

SSAASI My toughness is out.

OMO *spits.*

KADOGO Your rotten stomach spoils the air, the boy spits - lick it!

SSAASI My life is a crime. Punish.

OMO Why don't we just find something easier to eat?

SSAASI Because I was born with a face for him to hate.

KADOGO Hate is nothing. Your face is a face of death.

SSAASI That is accident of birth.

KADOGO Say that to your tribe!

Again KADOGO*'s haunted nature resurfaces.*

SSAASI If this is my life, this is my life. Tell me what you want, and I'll do it!

KADOGO Fine, one of the two: lick that away, or eat your 'cowboyness.'

OMO Not for my sins. (*Erases spit with his foot*). Now you have one thing.

KADOGO Omo, don't rub out your luck. Ssaasi, respect your words.

SSAASI I'm hungry, really, but not for cloth.

KADOGO Eat your words.

OMO Look we could just throw this cowboy stuff away. It stinks!

SSAASI That is my life you are talking about!

OMO *throws it to the ground.*

KADOGO Pick it up! Do not make me join you together.

OMO *does as ordered.*

KADOGO Senior fool, eat or be eaten. Junior fool, feed him.

OMO I'm sorry.

SSAASI Save me your mouth, and do as the man says!

OMO *puts shirt in* SSAASI'S *mouth. At that time, jubilation from without!*

OMO *dashes over to see.* KADOGO *goes to the radio.* SSAASI *is left there, shirt in mouth.* OMO *sings GO TELL IT ON THE MOUNTAINS as* SSAASI *lets shirt fall and tries to draw his attention, because known to only* SSAASI, *his I.D card – the one he denied having - has dropped!*

OMO Go tell it on the mountains...

SSAASI Omo...!

OMO Over the hills and every where...

SSAASI Omoding...!

OMO Go tell it on the mountains ...

SSAASI Friend...!

OMO The wonders God has done...

SSAASI Brother...!

KADOGO Shut up!

SSAASI *shoots down to the ground, to hide the dreaded card.*

KADOGO News report says peace-talks successful. President Milambo and rebel leader Mukamtagara shook hands. That is peace jokes! I tell you one of them is doing something the other cannot see.

OMO But how can you tell?

KADOGO If time proves me wrong, cut off my right hand.

OMO (*Close to crying*). God - This whole war business... The rest of life goes by...Us, we are looking at one thing war... Mother of God pray for us sinners, now and at the hour of our death!

KADOGO This would be a good place to die.

Silence.

OMO Sssasi?

SSAASI Me?

OMO You called me for what?

SSAASI No. I did not.

KADOGO You called him! I heard...and why did you go down like that?

SSAASI Your voice...when you said 'shut up,' it-it was l-l-like thunder.

KADOGO You must see a child, when you look at me.

Pushes him over with foot. Picks card from under SSAASI.

SSAASI I can explain!

KADOGO See this! Why am I not surprised? Read this Omo.

OMO Toto! Toto!

KADOGO I don't see your mother there, read.

SSAASI I am not the one.

KADOGO That face. (*Kicks SSAASI in the belly*). Do you know how much time I spent worrying about your face? Omo read.

SSAASI Please...!

OMO Mukamtagara.

KADOGO All the time, your face...eating me; now I know.

OMO Mukamtagara is signing peace.

KADOGO The same name -

40

SSAASI That there is not me, here!

KADOGO Almost the same face!

SSAASI The truth is with me.

OMO What truth! I fear you so much if I was the one with the gun – I fear for you.

SSAASI Omo, he is my brother, the one of the grass roof. But I'm not him. He is not me...

When the army rustled our neighbour's cattle, he got angry, and picked a gun saying he is going to put things right. He went into the bush, and like that, he had become a rebel. I did not... I refused...

KADOGO I refuse your lies.

SSAASI My father and mother, before they went to the grave, told my brother and me never to pick the gun. That those who live by the sword, die by the sword. I had already dropped out school; I feared to let them down, again. Don't make me like this...

KADOGO *does that menacing 'one to ten' tune of his.*

KADOGO Time to go.

OMO Where?

SSAASI Yes, where?

KADOGO Out of here! (*Starts to drag him*).

OMO With me, I can't leave.

SSAASI *and Mr Death meet again.*

SSAASI You are leaving me to die! Remember death, Omo? Don't leave me now.

OMO You lied to me about your name.

KADOGO You lied about not having an identity card.

SSAASI Fear. An identity card - with that name? You would shoot me! Straight.

KADOGO You don't know me!

SSAASI You have heard with your own ears. Now follow - and see - with your own eyes.

OMO I neither believe my eyes, nor my ears.

KADOGO Snake, move.

KADOGO gets his talismans and bites upon them. For SSAASI, this is surely his time.

SSAASI I would do the same for you.

OMO I don't know who you are.

SSAASI I'm Ssaasi!

OMO You could be Napoleon, Bokassa, Amin or Hitler.

SSAASI Mukamtagara - brother of Mukamtagara - if you want!

OMO Which one is you?

SSAASI I'm the man you shared your fear with... Omo... Omoding...I'm me! Every body lies... You also lied... Remember; remember saying you hate seeing a man being dragged to his death...!

He is dragged off.

Blackout.

ACT TWO

Scene One

Afternoon. Rain-storm, thunder and lightning, from without the cave. Scribbled on the walls of the cave are the words: 'MY TINA, PLEASE WAIT HERE, YOUR OMO.' OMO is seated, folded up. Before him a bunch of bananas. He is at the task of eating a couple of bananas. Thinking. He pushes bananas aside. Throws cowboy T-shirt, which covers the bananas... He kneels: makes sign of the cross, decides otherwise, gets up, goes to erase the wording, using banana peels.

OMO Tina... I, Omoding, would face this rain - or anything, for you... Where are you...?

You are the one who said not to be brave. To run, run, run. Up to this place. Then, together, we shall run... I followed your plan... I risked all... I am here. Do I now wait forever? Don't make me give up, Tina... Appear!

Thunder. Lightning. Rain. A helmet is tossed in.

OMO Toto...!

KADOGO Omo... Alone...? (*But* OMO *offers no reply*). Answer...! If you are alone, throw back that helmet; if nothing, I come in firing!

OMO is propelled into running over, and tossing the helmet toward the direction from which it was thrown in. Enter KADOGO, *wet and muddy.*

KADOGO You are still here; I have come for one thing.

OMO What thing?

He goes past OMO.

KADOGO And I'm leaving -

Something makes KADOGO *stop.*

Smell of bananas!

OMO *uncovers them from under cowboy T- shirt, but holds onto them like a selfish child.*

OMO They are my bananas.

KADOGO I want some.

OMO I risked my life! Trusting the Mother of God, I dashed out of here -

KADOGO You went out there?

OMO Hail Mary on my lips.

KADOGO You came back in here?

OMO Holy Mary on my lips; but in my hands, bananas.

KADOGO Big 'why,' and I want a big 'because.'

OMO This where my girl told me to meet her.

KADOGO Tell me bananas not women.

OMO Hunger. Dying of hunger is also fearsome.

KADOGO I'm hungry.

OMO Be.

KADOGO Don't say, 'be.' Offer.

OMO I was not offered, I barter traded a watch!

KADOGO What is a watch?

Removes the one on his wrist and tosses it over.

OMO (*Shaking it*) Fake. (*Retrieves bananas*). An old woman gave the bananas to me – not for nothing, for my watch.

KADOGO Wait. Let me see. (*Shakes and examines it couple of times.*) Ssaasi stole, I grabbed, it jams. (*Throws it away*). What do I have left now?

OMO Nothing.

KADOGO Except the gun.

OMO Guns and me, no way. Keep your gun; I keep my bananas.

KADOGO Foolish boy.

44

OMO What is God's is God's. What is for Caesar is for Caesar.

KADOGO Now I know why Hondo shot that cigarette boy.

OMO Kadogo, eat - all!

OMO *surrenders the bananas.* KADOGO *begins to eat the bananas.*

KADOGO Food is life and death, like the gun.

OMO Kadogo, please don't kill me: not for bananas, not for Ssaasi. Bananas, I have given you. Ssaasi, I don't know. I don't want to be next. You killed the man, you killed him.

KADOGO Fool.

OMO Complete fool that man.

KADOGO Not him, you.

Beat.

OMO Give me a chance to make peace with God first.

KADOGO This gun. (*Lowers gun*).

OMO I'm grateful. (*Kneels*).

KADOGO No, no, my friend...

OMO Only one little prayer like this.

KADOGO You think I am going to kill you because -

OMO You think I might reveal it. But let's make a deal. You and me.

KADOGO Did you see the man die?

OMO My life: and what happened becomes our dying secret.

KADOGO Did you see me shoot him?

OMO I will not. I refuse from here; I'll not betray you for a dead fellow.

KADOGO Are you in a position to point at his body?

OMO The dead belong to the dead.

KADOGO You know nothing about me.

OMO Completely. I am no witness -

KADOGO Close your mouth and listen! 'Witness' – did you witness the man being killed by me? Look at his mouth. Open like a hole. So what if I killed him? Last war, our tribe saw days! Where were you? That Ssaasi, people from his area invaded our home. They did to my father things...

Everything I did today, they did to my father! I once had parents... But now – you are looking at the world's biggest orphan. Go and thank that man Ssaasi's tribe!

OMO In my next life, I'll refuse to be born unless I can choose a tribe.

KADOGO My father said all that! But the gang replied. 'You can be any tribe you want Mister, we are here to make you eat your words.' Be what you are – my father was a teacher, who sometimes criticised government system. What did government do? They gave him a job. Simply. He changed his song: proposed life presidency for the man in the chair, and even threatened to eat his shirt, if such a perfect presidency, a perfect gift from none but God, ended before twenty years. The government was overthrown; Ssaasi's tribe made him eat his shirt!

OMO Sickness!

KADOGO When my mother tried to plead, worse things happened... (*The haunting returns*).Things that have been making my head go this way and that since...

OMO I understand.

KADOGO My actions on that ...er...Ssaasi, Mukamtagara: that was for my father.

OMO And mother -

KADOGO I'm not going to tell you my whole life!

Silence.

And you are worrying about that professional crook... I had to struggle for my life. He ran away; that was my escape! Look at my neck; look. This is an animal...

KADOGO Don't even know how I still have my gun. Here I am. This is mud; not blood.

OMO I see...

46

KADOGO It is him who nearly killed me. Nobody killed, or got killed.

OMO So Ssaasi is alive?

KADOGO You want him, you go out there. You find him, you ask him! My plan was to find soldiers, who could deal with him…

OMO Why didn't you just shoot him?

KADOGO I have not come to answer to you; I have come to go.

OMO Kadogo, where?

KADOGO I don't know…

   Beat.

Dying is not for me. I must run out of this country.

OMO To which country?

KADOGO Any that is at peace – don't care which.

OMO The money?

   KADOGO *spreads his hands to indicate the lack of it.*

Are you going to grow wings?

KADOGO These legs; they can walk from here to the end!

OMO But…look at you…that combat.

KADOGO All I need is a dead body, and I have found civilian clothing.

OMO Undressing the dead? Wickedness!

KADOGO You want me to undress you!

OMO Kadogo –

KADOGO Because whether you 'Kadogo' me a thousand times, I must go. Hell is coming.

I cannot be here waiting for death.

OMO You are the one going out to meet it.

KADOGO I don't care!

OMO You do; that is this hiding.

KADOGO Whatever is coming will find me somewhere else!

OMO With luck -

KADOGO You boy, luck and me don't meet! I don't know what happened, but luck?

Me? We quarrelled. Badly... I'm out of this cave -

OMO That might be a mistake.

KADOGO The government is losing! Why are you making me shout? That is the only reason that dictator, General Milambo would accept talks. His big speech: 'I want to assure this nation, we shall follow rebels in the bush and leave them there,' is now full of holes, like the walls of this town. Mukamtagara, the rebel is going to exploit the cease-fire; and fulfil his ambition to become the President.

OMO You are not God.

KADOGO This is up to General Milambo, and Rebel Mukamtagara - not God!

Silence. The rain comes to an end...

KADOGO After the rain always comes something!

OMO What is going to come now?

KADOGO You stay and find out!

OMO (*Holds on to* KADOGO). Stop scaring me!

KADOGO Stop holding me!

OMO Let me confess: better when you are in here with somebody. Don't leave me.

KADOGO I cannot stay! If you want, follow me.

OMO I want to, but - God, end this!

KADOGO Omo, we are going out there. If we make it, good. If not, we tried. If you don't, I go on. If I don't, (*Raises the gun*), this is what you need!

OMO I am not a gunman.

KADOGO I can teach you how to shoot a gun.

OMO Toto…!

KADOGO I won't tell your mother.

OMO Kadogo: guns and me, no. In our village, there was a training camp. By secret I used to watch the training, from a rock. Hidden. I'll never forget what I saw one day. Our neighbour's son, by accident, shot the instructor. Poor boy was chased, caught, shot.

KADOGO Foolish instructor. First remove the magazine. (*Does so, and puts it in the pocket*). No magazine, no bullets. Then, cork. Like this…one hand here…one hand trigger…shoot.

In time of alert, keep safety catch on. Sign of danger, remove catch…

   Click.

OMO Menacing!

KADOGO Fire! (*Offers gun*). Try?

OMO Be serious!

KADOGO Each corking: bullet in, bullet out. In, out. Like this, like that; quarra-quarra.

OMO To handle a gun is to handle death.

KADOGO If you fear death, let's go.

OMO Can we wait?

KADOGO 'We?' Sorry, bye.

OMO I am on my knees, please.

KADOGO You wait; I go.

OMO One more night?

KADOGO Waiting for -?

OMO My friend - my girlfriend.

KADOGO I thought I was looking at some wise boy running for his life. All along you are some fool. A fool for a woman.

OMO Just one night. Tomorrow we go.

KADOGO What if there is no tomorrow?

Silence. KADOGO *pushes* OMO *out of the way, and goes toward his place in the cave.* OMO *talks after him.*

OMO Have you ever loved a girl?

KADOGO There is no girl worth loving!

OMO Wrong. I love Tina.

KADOGO Love her... But if something happened to you, that Nina -

OMO Tina -

KADOGO Will she be there?

OMO Far as I know.

KADOGO You don't know women.

OMO You don't know Tina.

KADOGO How much did your Tina, 'tina' you?

OMO Tina and I were the best at history. We decided to come to the cave, to see a place Stone Age people occupied. Even if rumours said this cave has ghosts. Each time, however, there were no ghosts.

KADOGO Except hers, and yours?

OMO I like that! One day boy-ghost asked girl-ghost to visit him at his home, reassuring her he does not rape. Girl ghost shyly answered that she was not scared of him raping her, because she knew he was not like that. Her fear was one. She was afraid there would be no need for a rape, and she wasn't ready for that yet.

KADOGO So sweet.

OMO Some women can be sweet.

KADOGO Then girl ghost and boy ghost?

OMO Then the eyes met.

KADOGO Then?

OMO Eyes got into trouble.

KADOGO Then?

OMO Hands got into trouble.

50

KADOGO Then?

OMO Our everywhere else got into trouble.

KADOGO Ho! Ho!

OMO And that day, what happened in this cave is too scandalous for words! Unforgetten. Unforgettable. That spot…us two were there – ashamed but fulfilled – when she said, 'Everyone is talking war. If war happens, do not be brave. Run. Run to this place. I'll do the same. And together we shall keep running…'My being here is her. I will wait.

KADOGO Stupid boy; there is no woman worth waiting for.

OMO One day you'll find one.

KADOGO One day - school days - I did. There are women and women, but I saw this girl…The world turned. I loved her. I died a little for her. I wanted her. I feared her. I -

OMO Fine, fine, you 'everythinged' her.

KADOGO Who is telling whom? Listen. Once, I was at the school gate, she appeared!

You know appeared?

OMO You want me to spell it?

KADOGO My heart: tu-tum, tu-tum, tu-tum. She smiled!

OMO What did you say?

KADOGO A vision.

OMO What you said, not what you saw! Okay, what did you say to this vision of yours.

KADOGO *barks as he did then.*

OMO Wait, wait. Do not get carried away. I want to know -

KADOGO That is what I did.

OMO *barks like* KADOGO *did, in question form.* KADOGO *affirms, with same bark.*

OMO Like some dog?

KADOGO Like anything.

OMO And her?

KADOGO *screams as she did then.*

KADOGO And like that, we fell in love. One day she came home, to me give a present -

OMO A present, or the present?

KADOGO A tape.

OMO Oh…

KADOGO She tells me that whenever I play it: her, and me, we'll be together. Like magic.

I played it there and then. My mouth, as we danced, it started pouring things I did not know were in me. Telling her it was the song of my life, the song of always, the only song...

And, little by little, she ended up on my bed.

OMO On the bed, or in the bed?

KADOGO Not sex. This desire of my heart was lying there. So, so beautiful. Too beautiful. I have never seen anything like that.

OMO Did you, or didn't you?

KADOGO I said something I have not yet forgiven myself for.

OMO I want you?

KADOGO No.

OMO Let's make love?

KADOGO No.

OMO Do you mind if I close that door?

KADOGO No.

OMO Have you ever done it before?

KADOGO No.

OMO If you are telling, tell!

KADOGO AMAR AKBAR ANTHONY is showing. Let me treat you to a movie.

OMO Ha, ha.

KADOGO She said, 'hm, up to you.'

OMO He, He.

KADOGO We marched, as the town watched.

OMO Hi, Hi.

KADOGO My feet and spirit, in the air.

OMO Ho, Ho.

KADOGO Laugh, because she said, 'I bring you a special present, but - you prefer Indian films.'

OMO Hu, Hu!

KADOGO Not laughing, I protest from here to anywhere! I beg to forget the film. I declare films rubbish! Any film ever made. All films!

OMO But the real truth?

KADOGO Truth - I like films! Ever since. But see what they are doing to me now!

I find myself saying loudly, 'rubbish!' That is when a man stopped a bicycle – a sport bike-

OMO Sports, sports bike- sorry not a school...

KADOGO He came at us. Waving a threatening finger. He shouted: 'Do you think I am a civilian like you?' His eyes loaded with anger. Reflecting terror. A dark horrifying anger. An anger of all angers. 'Run,' my inside says to me, but how? I'm out with a princess!

From nowhere, a pistol! On my nose! The street is watching... Then, he released a slap!

OMO Bastard.

KADOGO A slap made in hell.

OMO Mean animal.

KADOGO He marched off, daring me to call him rubbish again.

OMO That is when I can chew somebody!

KADOGO But you see I had said rubbish to the girl!

OMO I know

KADOGO People standing there saying things like, 'That man's other name must be slap.'

'That slap is a world record... If slaps were money, that guy would die a millionaire... The slap! It can crack a rock'

OMO That is people for you.

KADOGO All the the vicious creatures of this world: lions, rhinos, tigers, crocodiles, snakes, wasps, bees – I tell you all; entered me. My head, it stopped working until I had been recruited in the army. On the day of pass out, all I wanted was a gun. To come back, kill the thug; finish the story by shooting myself!

OMO Sometimes life takes a person down there.

KADOGO Gun corked and ready, I went for my mission. But when I got there, it was drinking time, so most men were away. Okay, I'll ask for his drinking joint, and target him from there. Neighbour says, 'how do I know? Every house here sells booze. This whole area is one large bar. Go ask the one he shares a bed with' I went to ask. I knocked. A pregnant woman opened...

OMO And told you the drinking place?

KADOGO No...

OMO Refused to tell you; smelling a rat?

KADOGO It was the desire of my heart!

OMO To-to! Do not say you shot her.

KADOGO No...! How could I shoot her?

OMO What of your man?

KADOGO How could I shoot him...? How could I shoot anything? You shoot when there is something to shoot for. And for me, what was there? What was left to shoot? Pain...? She was there – pregnant; I was there – poisonous! She was there...nothing, but the ugliest thing I had ever seen.

OMO I hear that is called the thin line.

KADOGO Somehow, I turned. I walked away; somehow.

OMO Our man!

KADOGO She took action!

From this point, he is 'two people,' himself and her.

Follows me from the beginning of the barracks to the end – I'm walking. She is wild like an animal with new babies - I'm still walking. Her mouth spits fire - I keep walking: "You are going to walk away like that? Saying nothing? You know you refused to listen to me. Remember... Remember how I begged. But: stupid, angry, childish you went to the army anyway. You wanted revenge. Not me. You made a choice. I said if you go; I go. I tried to threaten you. I told you 'if you go I'll take the first man who approaches me.' Do you recall what you said?" She hits me. 'Do you?' Hits again. 'You said you don't care! And that same man, your man, approached me - first. Came to me, really sorry, apologised for his bad manners. Then took my hand, looked me in the eyes, and said if I were to let him into my heart, he would never slap again. So, I also kept my bitter promise to you.' Hits again and again. 'Him. You. What is the difference? Show me. Show me, Olatunde...'

Pause.

Women - I have been there. What again can you tell me?

OMO Mistake wasn't to love the girl: but to join the army, for the wrong reasons.

KADOGO I asked to quit; they refused. The army does not let go easily. Once you are in, you are in. I was in. Olatunde had become Kadogo.

OMO Ola-tu-nde! So that is your name...

KADOGO This Kadogo thing I picked up in the army - for my smallness. But now I am a deserter. The spirit that took me to the army died. The spirit for women, no more. The only spirit left is the one, which wants to be me; the 'me' I was.

OMO My literature teacher was small, but her heart, her spirit, made her the biggest person you could find.

KADOGO That spirit of mine is not ashamed to be running for its life.

OMO Run.

KADOGO To be hiding.

OMO Hide.

KADOGO To be committing treason.

OMO Ugh my friend, look at whom is fighting whom. No noble cause. It is only treason if it is against your country. Not against mindless warlords.

KADOGO The spirit of Olatunde is running for life. If government troops find me, treason. Rebels find me, enemy. Real hostage situation!

Pause

Omo, I came for what is mine. That radio.

OMO ushers him on, but as he goes for the radio -

OMO Kadogo, what does Olatunde mean?

KADOGO Honour comes again.

OMO You could start from that point.

KADOGO I try so hard. (*laughs*) Funny. Those are Ssaasi's words.

OMO (*laughs*) Oh yes! (*laughs*) What Ssaasi didn't know, is that this honourable, eats people's bananas, using a gun, to avoid paying.

KADOGO Mother of my father!

OMO That - that gun trick, that is honourable!

KADOGO Are you still talking about those bananas!

OMO Didn't you put terror in us with that gun? Didn't you use it on my bananas? Now even a joke about it is a sin?

KADOGO If it is joke, it smells.

OMO It is a joke, it smells, you ate my hard earned bananas.

KADOGO Hard earned!

OMO Cost me a whole watch.

KADOGO I gave you that watch off Ssaasi.

OMO It was a fake watch.

KADOGO Looted things!

OMO You could have given me something else.

56

KADOGO Come and suck my blood.

OMO Something of value.

KADOGO I have no money!

OMO Something like – that radio…

KADOGO The - you think - (*storms off*)! No wonder my stomach is paining. Where I come from, when you give someone something – especially something to eat – don't create a song!

OMO (*Musing*). Was that giving?

KADOGO Bananas, bananas, bananas. (*stuffs radio into* OMO'S *hands*). Radio, radio, radio.

> *But,* OMO *is struck by something about the radio, and puts it down quickly.*

OMO No.

KADOGO No what! I forgot to kneel?

OMO I cannot.

KADOGO No, take it, if you think life is a radio.

OMO That radio, it speaks to me – almost.

KADOGO You boy, this radio was okay when I left. If anything is wrong, you.

> *Snaps it on. Music, as* OMO *stands there, shaking his head.*

That is music.

OMO Oh no…

KADOGO If I didn't know you, I would have said you are deaf. These ears of mine hear music.

OMO Perhaps…

KADOGO Perhaps? Per-what? Perhaps you want me to dance. (*Dances*) Mr 'Toto,' is it music now? I can dance up to sweating blood. You like this? Or that? Or quarra-quarra?

OMO (*To self*) I know that radio…! (*Turns off the music*). Friend of mine owned that radio.

KADOGO Now, I do.

OMO I gave it to her!

KADOGO I got it from her!

OMO picks up gun and knocks KADOGO *over. Keeps trying to shoot him.*

Realising it is futile he attacks KADOGO *and tries to strangle him with gun.* KADOGO *gets out of grip with gun advantage.*

KADOGO Let me show you.

OMO Yes! Yes! Nothing matters now. Do it. Shoot! Fire! What a good way to end. Papa and toto, you are the best parents. Tina, I love you. Hail Mary, here I come!

KADOGO regards him for a while. When OMO *comes to,* KADOGO *has backed off.*

KADOGO How will it ever end? Stupid me encouraged you to take the gun. First person in your eyes, you want to shoot.

Removes magazine and this time exposes.

KADOGO This gun you see, friend Omo, carries no bullets... I use it to scare. A deserter soon runs out of bullets. I had to find a trick. Now I am glad it is empty... I could have been your first victim. And I thought you were the good one... Why...?

OMO First I apologise.

KADOGO That is not my interest.

OMO Then I ask -

KADOGO Answer mine, then ask yours.

OMO Because if I don't - if you don't - if we don't clear this, in this cave, anything can happen.

KADOGO Turn into a dog if you really want to scare me.

OMO There are two kinds of dogs. The one that folds its tail and runs from trouble, and the other that shoots ears up and runs toward trouble. I belong to the second kind.

KADOGO Turn your mouth into action.

OMO It is not your size; not your this, not your that, not your 'quarra-quarra.'

KADOGO Oh, it's your toto! Sorry, your mother doesn't scare me.

They regard each other.

OMO Look, deep inside, I do not like trouble; but there is a point, where the animal in me comes out.

KADOGO 'Toto!' What a threat! And I have no mother to run to.

OMO This is real! As real as what I found when I went to check if my papa and toto had survived the war. Graves, for friends. Nearly all the boys and girls I grew up playing with. Now Tina as well? No. You are looking at someone whose life is worthless.

KADOGO But what demon tells you I'm the one who killed those friends...!

OMO I ask you, like person to person...

KADOGO Which one is the real you: the person or the animal?

OMO Where is Tina?

KADOGO Under my armpits!

OMO That gun is empty.

KADOGO Like you.

OMO Plain. Simple. Where-is-Tina? (*Picks up radio*). I gave this radio to a girl. You say a girl gave this radio to you. This hand you see here, this my hand, wrote these words: 'with permanent love, to dearest Tina.'

KADOGO Mine was Christina.

OMO Yours! You said yours! Please don't say that.

KADOGO What do you want me to say? The girl I got it from...that poor girl, she was Christina.

OMO And the world needs a school built for you alone, to work out one is the other... Christina was Omoding's Tina, as Omoding was Tina's Omo. She baptised me Omo, I baptised her Tina.

KADOGO Dark girl?

OMO Black beauty.

KADOGO Short hair?

OMO Natural.

KADOGO Large eyes?

OMO Those are her eyes!

KADOGO White teeth?

OMO Like milk.

KADOGO I will not add to the pain. I know not where she is.

OMO No, tell me the worst.

KADOGO Omoding -

OMO Ugh!

KADOGO Please I do not want to remember that time, and its ugliness!

OMO I swear, I want you to remember...

KADOGO It was something code-named, 'Operation College.' Some diseased soldiers I was with raided Valley college, set the boys on fire, and raped: girl to girl.

OMO Kill me. Otherwise, I'll hunt you till the end, as long as either of us lives...

KADOGO I tried not to tell you.

OMO Let me use the best words possible: did you, or didn't you?

KADOGO I'm not like that!

OMO You had her.

KADOGO Not me!

OMO I want to die.

KADOGO When it was my turn...I could not! I grabbed the radio; nothing more –

OMO Today is when I die; kill me!

KADOGO Apart from helping her escape!

OMO You want me to believe you.

KADOGO Not for her, for my mother! Do you know how or why my mother died? She suffered that... The thugs who attacked home: three-of-them...! There, in front of my father and me! You don't know anything about me, so do not call me a rapist!

My father; he refused my mother! My mother; she bought poison, and used it. You think I enjoyed that? Or what I discovered in the garage? My father – hanging from a tie my mother actually bought for him. He left a little letter: 'Madness has invaded this home.' I cannot again go on that way! I let that girl go in honour of my mother. From that time, I felt my mother's soul rest.

OMO *heaves a large sigh.*

OMO Some people better bitter experiences.

KADOGO I do what I do for good - many times I fail.

OMO I want those beasts!

KADOGO Same mistake I made.

OMO Anything that will provide a gun, I swear to join. Army, rebels – whatever the case maybe!

KADOGO If you join something for the wrong reasons, there will be a lack of discipline for it. Then you, and all, will suffer.

OMO I wish your gun had bullets - I'll find one; I'll also find those dogs!

And he sets about it, but KADOGO *restrains him.*

KADOGO As we talk now, they are not here! They are where you want to go! Probably eating Satan's left overs... And let that be a warning to us all.

OMO Which good devil came for them?

KADOGO Three nights later, fellows created time to 'forget the war,' a little bit. They grabbed that same radio you see there: played it, joked, laughed... Dancing like they will never die... It just happened! A mean bundle of rebels attacked. Ten: against all those, we automatically put down our guns in surrender. They asked for the owner of the radio. The other nine quickly pointed at me, denying anything about everything. I denied the bloody radio, saying it belonged to a girl... One of the rebels said, 'he

must be the one.' It took five of them to get me to a corner. I was
fighting, kicking, crying – praying. Clinging to life… Starting
with the legs, they shot.

OMO Come on, you are standing on normal legs -

KADOGO They shot not me, the others! The nine who had
messed Tina.

OMO The nine swine!

KADOGO They were left to bleed to death - slowly. 'Join us,'
the rebels offered three times. I had no mouth to answer. I could
only shiver in that corner, mucus running like a downhill river.
The rebels left me there. I knew, from deep inside me, I had left
the army… I did not ask anybody's permission. I did not need it.
I kept walking till I found this cave.

It is a time to either stay or go.

OMO Christina, Tina: tell me where she went to…if you know.

KADOGO Into the night.

*Silence. Nothing more to be said. It becomes clear between
them* KADOGO *must go as indeed* OMO *must stay – a time
for departure.* KADOGO *looks back and forth from radio to*
OMO…*decides to leave it.* OMO *reacts by giving it to him.*

KADOGO *takes a moment to decide. He accepts it.* OMO
*offers handshake, but with gun in one hand, and radio in
another,* KADOGO *can only return fore-arm in this parting
ritual.*

A sudden outburst of war-exchange. OMO *curiously wants to
see what is going on.* KADOGO *hits the ground for cover.*

Take cover! Down! Down! Down!

He rushes over, yanks OMO *to the ground!*

In a time of fire, stay down!

*Stray bullet hits him. He reacts slowly to it all. Seats in a
crouched position, apart from* OMO, *who imitates the way he
is seated. Both are in some kind of trance.*

The fighting continues.

OMO The end of the world is here.

KADOGO Omo...you are how old?

OMO Nineteen.

KADOGO Me, twenty-seven and about to die. Can you believe that?

OMO Do not lose hope. To lose hope is to embrace evil. I just hope for a time of sanity; but we shall survive. We'll have children. And I promise to tell my children not to kill your children.

KADOGO I am the only child of my father and mother... My father was the only child of his father and mother... My mother was the only child of her father and mother. We called ourselves, 'the only ones.' Mr. Only one, Mrs. Only one, and Junior Only one... But now, the whole clan is about to be wiped out.

OMO You were right; we should have left...

KADOGO Come here, Omo.

OMO Here, there, does it matter? Death is spread.

KADOGO This is no time to argue!

OMO Kadogo, shout at the people fighting, not me.

KADOGO I have been shot!

OMO What...? (*Gets up to go and see*).

KADOGO Down, stay down! (OMO *takes ground cover*) Do you want to die?

   Silence.

OMO Kadogo! (*Crawls over and shakes him.*) Laugh, cry, shout – Olatunde!

KADOGO I am still here.

OMO Do not keep quiet; it scares!

OMO (*Sees where* KADOGO *has been hit*) Toto! Toto! You, my friend, die of my death. You took my bullet. Look, I am the creep; why did you bother to pull me down?

KADOGO Stop the blood.

OMO Let me tie you; I have to use Ssaasi's T-shirt-

KADOGO It will help.

OMO *gets it, and uses it, as* KADOGO *whimpers. The fighting ceases.*

KADOGO Dizzy…Fever…

OMO Ceaseless wars! Us against Us!

Makes sign of the cross.

Hail Ma – Lord; by whatever means, eradicate war - no, banish warlords!

(*Blood on* OMO'*S hands*).

This is my blood! Do you see this, God? Can you hear me?

KADOGO Leave now, if you want to survive.

OMO Not unless you are coming with me.

KADOGO I will be a burden.

OMO I don't desert my friends in this fashion.

KADOGO Nice. Not wise.

OMO Don't preach!

He goes to spy on what is happening – people running up and down - He returns.

OMO Going is death; staying is death.

From the outside: the sharp screaming of a woman, competes with the laughing of a man. They run into the distance. A shot in the air. Laughter.

KADOGO You better start running.

OMO Out of the question.

KADOGO Go!

OMO No!

KADOGO I said go!

OMO I said no!

KADOGO You want to end up like me?

OMO I want to slap that mouth of yours!

64

Checks himself in time not to.

KADOGO Slap, but I see danger.

OMO This, this place here, this bloody place…is where danger of any size, or colour, or shape, will find us then. Like this. You and me. Together.

KADOGO What good are two dead bodies?

Silence.

Oh ancestors…

KADOGO *is gone, as* OMO *establishes when he three times raises* KADOGO'S *hand and three times it drops, in a fatal manner.*

SSAASI (*off*) Hands up all of you. It is over.

OMO *remains unmoved, and ignores* SSAASI. *He rests* KADOGO *down.* SSAASI *enters with gun - a pistol worn cowboy style, and gum-boots, still in the same jeans, a fancy jacket, but with an army beret.*

Hands up before I shoot. Mikono juu!

Still ignoring 'the intruder' OMO *makes sign of the cross.*

The gun, I want that gun!

OMO *makes room for* SSAASI *to take the gun.* OMO, *unshaken, chooses to pray. But as he does this,* SSAASI *sings. Whereas this is done at the same level,* OMO *aims to pacify* KADOGO'S *soul,* SSAASI *aims to taunt it!* OMO *recites the second part of HAIL MARY,* SSAASI *sings GO TELL IT ON THE MOUNTAINS. .*

SSAASI Brave boy.

OMO I didn't kill him.

SSAASI As if I care.

OMO He was caught in cross-fire.

SSAASI Everything ends. Even Kadogo! Death; death is the thing! Where were his talisman things?

OMO Unearth your father and mother; perhaps they have the answer!

Silence.

SSAASI That hurt.

OMO I hope so.

SSAASI *threatens* OMO *with gun on the head again.*

SSAASI That really hurt.

OMO I really hope so.

SSAASI Don't go there again!

OMO I'm waiting... Shoot!

SSAASI *hits* OMO *with knuckles on the head.*

SSAASI Traitor. But, you saved my life many times. Whether you knew or not, you saved me – until the last minute, when you washed your hands – but...I forgive you.

OMO See him. Thinking that gun makes him God - rebel all along.

SSAASI Who says? When I ran from that little nothing, I fell into rebels! They want to rough me, but I use the name Mukamtagara. They take me to check. It is my brother's wife – in combat! She says it is true my story. I am her brother-in-law. They show me how to cock (*does so*), shoot! (*Actually fires*). They hand me a gun. I just joined today. Out there, we are marching into the city. We are the new liberators.

OMO Look at you. Look at us. Look at this country. So this is what we get?

SSAASI This is what we get what?

OMO You wake up as...you know what you were – the sun has not even gone down, you are a so-called liberator!

SSAASI And more liberators are still needed. I can take you to be recruited - like that. Joining takes a minute. Time to change things in this country.

OMO Another Animal Farm?

SSAASI If you want a farm of animals, no sweat. Main man is my brother. Chance of your life. Riches from now on, I tell you.

OMO Thank you, but - N, O.

SSAASI You saw with your own eyes what happened to me.

OMO Shall I take out my eyes?

SSAASI Take your chance to become powerful like nothing!

OMO If we all become gunmen, what will become of life?

SSAASI Life? I see very little in here. Only a dead body and a half.

OMO For people who have reached where I have, death is just another word.

SSAASI And life is another one. We go.

OMO What about him?

SSAASI Let him come if he can walk.

OMO Look at you. I despise you. I'm talking about burying him - at least.

SSAASI Using what to dig? That helmet? This gun? Your hands, or your teeth!

OMO This man deserves decent last respects!

SSAASI That was not my reason of returning to this cave.

OMO You had come to kill him.

SSAASI I...think so, yes.

OMO I tried to murder him; you return to kill him.

SSAASI I had come to show him the animal he created.

OMO Bleeding others is bleeding ourselves.

SSAASI I had come to urinate on him.

OMO Poor man was scared like you and me.

SSAASI To spit in his mouth.

OMO He played tough for his own sake!

SSAASI To make him taller.

OMO So sickeningly sad.

SSAASI Be there thinking you can make me care for that man.
Be there thinking anything can.

OMO He is dead; you are alive!

SSAASI You think because he loved me?

If I hadn't cried for a toilet. If he had not been foolish to believe me. If I had not stayed in the toilet up to when he came to check. If I hadn't hidden up, like a commando - a cowboy. If I had not attacked when he reached the door. I would not be here. I would be down. Below. Trying to lie to my father why I left school. With my mother saying: 'leave the boy.' If I had not played suicide…!

OMO See that gun, it carried no bullets even!

SSAASI (*Checks it*) If I had known! If I had known!

OMO And I wish to bury him, even if it kills me.

SSAASI Wake up, Omo. War is war. People die. Get out and see. I came here jumping over dead bodies. I counted sixty-four! Sixty-four! Like that. One time. Like nothing. Gone. All fresh. Bury your man. After him, go and bury them all. I challenge you. Even if you bury morning and afternoon. You need thirty whole days. Thirty like this. That is a month. Unless you can manage a mass grave…

OMO You must have been born feet first. And the pity is, your parents could have gone around proclaiming they had got a child. I see Lucifer.

SSAASI And you are here abusing me. This is just another body. Body sixty-five.

OMO Even what is left of him only, is better than you and I…

SSAASI That one is no better than Stone Age people.

OMO Empty talk from an empty head…

SSAASI *employs his knuckle again.*

You can do that, but say nothing about the Stone Age people. Those people knew how to live together. Hunt animals for food; we hunt each other. Make a good fire and share the warmth. Use it to keep away trouble from animals. We use it to burn innocent school children, and villages. Tell me what is primitive?

SSAASI Standing here to watch a dead body!

Starts to leave, gets to the exit, then...

Tell his silly little body how disappointed I'm at his death.
Dying with someone's debt is not fair. I had returned, for us to
measure manhood... I will take the radio.

OMO The radio - now that radio - it stays here. That is that.

They grab the radio back and forth.

SSAASI I don't think he bought it.

OMO It is his radio!

SSAASI See, he didn't hear you.

OMO He is dead Ssaasi! (*He now has radio, firmly*). Why don't
you let him be?

Okay, eat him and rest!

Silence.

SSAASI Use your eyes; he has my T-shirt.

OMO Ugh you took my socks!

SSAASI Then let me take his radio!

They hold it in struggle.

OMO To take this radio, you have to take my life first.

SSAASI Say you want it for you.

OMO Fool. See and hear things one way.

SSAASI Everyone is a fool sometimes. You have become a
foolish saint.

OMO And you a foolish liberator.

They lock a gaze.

SSAASI I'll take this radio, and wait for his ghost to come and
ask me why.

OMO I'll say this. And you may do what you want...

Apart from promoting yourself from thief to gunman, it seems
you really are determined to steal all your life. To die a thief -
even after all you stole.

SSAASI *pushes radio away in anger.*

SSAASI Okay arrest me! I stole. So? In your clan, in your line of blood: from your first grandfather to the last, was there not a thief? You come from a tribe that came from a tribe that steals cattle; and you are here opening your mouth to the end of the earth...Ugh, let me at least kick him!

OMO Kick him, and heaven and earth will meet.

SSAASI *continually attempts to kick* KADOGO*'S body, but each time* OMO *blocks.*

SSAASI He messed my life.

OMO He saved mine.

SSAASI He took my life away!

OMO He gave me mine!

SSAASI One kick! Only one – as little – as him. Out of my way!

He releases a kick similar to what he suffered at KADOGO*'S hands.*

The effects on OMO *are similar.*

SSAASI He made my life small! As small as himself. Over nothing. Too much.

And I should live with that? Take that to angels! I'm human.

OMO Who am I? I did not create this world. Kick him. Kick. Kick all you want. Kick him harder than he kicked you, or you me. Not once. Not seven times. But seventy-seven times. He might come back to life, and beg you for mercy.

Great ambition. Kicking the dead. I say this to you, Ssaasi - Mukamtagara - whatever your name is: if you do kick that man, that lifeless body, live forever. Do not die. You will not be accepted.

The dead will reject you.

Silence.

SSAASI Cowboy never die!

SSAASI *goes to* KADOGO'S *body. He rips off the talismans, sets them afire, jumps back and forth over the body, as he chants wildly. Random shooting from the outside,* OMO *is unmoved. Drumming and cheering and singing.*

SSAASI *tries to pull* OMO *away, in vain.*

SSAASI People are out there celebrating; you are in here loving a dead body.

OMO Out there is a cave, in here is my world!

SSAASI *suddenly screams, removes his jacket, ties it around the gun, runs to where he can see the outside, and joins the celebrations by making ululations.*

He talks back to OMO *at intervals.*

SSAASI Stop living in your head! (*Ululates*). There is more to life than what you see. What you cling on to. (*Chants*). Everything ends. Even this war... (*Cocks gun, shoots in the air*). Even that pain. I go with life as it comes. (*Jigs and cheers*). You, you don't know when to leave, when to stay. (*Raises both hands and waves wildly*).

The celebration fades. He returns to OMO.

Matter of choice. Staying, or coming...?

OMO *goes to* KADOGO. *He sets about resting one item after another upon his dead friend: gun, magazine, helmet, and radio - the only burial left in him.*

Stay. I'm gone.

As he exits, dogs howl from a distance, startling OMO.

Dogs... Just dogs.

OMO Dogs give me creeps...

SSAASI *exits.*

OMO Oh God...

OMO *turns on radio, which plays the song that* KADOGO *proclaimed as his 'life.'*

He exits. The light and the song fade slowly, with a focus on the body...and then out.

End.

An Instant Playscript

A Time of Fire first published in Great Britain in 1999
as a paperback original by Nick Hern Books Limited,
14 Larden Road, London W3 7ST in association with
Birmingham Repertory Theatre

Typeset by Country Setting, Kingsdown, Kent CT14 8ES

Printed and bound in Great Britain

ISBN 1 85459 478 8

A CIP catalogue record for this book is available from
the British Library